Learning About Invertebrates

By
DEBBIE ROUTH

COPYRIGHT © 2002 Mark Twain Media, Inc.

ISBN 1-58037-206-6

Printing No. CD-1552

Mark Twain Media, Inc., Publishers
Distributed by Carson-Dellosa Publishing Company, Inc.

Table of Contents

Introduction 1

Invertebrates: Eight Major Phyla 2

Animals: A Special Group of Organisms 3

    Vertebrate or Invertebrate? 3

    Symmetry 4

Keeping Track: Classification of Invertebrates 6

    What Is a Sponge? 8

        Crossword Puzzle 9

    What Is a Cnidarian? 10

    What Is a Flatworm? 12

    Other Flatworms 13

    What Is a Roundworm? 15

    What Is a Segmented Worm? 17

        Watching Worms Squirm: Constructing a Wormery 19

    What Is a Mollusk? 20

        Research: Mollusk Project 23

    What Is an Arthropod? 25

    What Is an Insect? 27

        Class Insecta 27

        How Do Insects Develop? 29

          All About Metamorphosis—Complete or Incomplete? 29

    Other Classes of Arthropods 31

    Name That Arthropod 33

    What Is an Echinoderm? 34

Invertebrates:

    Vocabulary: Study Sheet 36

    Word Web 37

    Kriss Kross 38

    Crossword Puzzle 39

    Unit Test 40

Answer Keys 42

Bibliography 46

Introduction

Welcome to a wonderful book that is devoted to the incredible invertebrates. *Learning About Invertebrates* is a book intended to help young zoologists discover all about the spineless members of the animal kingdom. The activities in this book will help guide student observers through the eight major **phyla** (groups) of invertebrates.

All of the animals in the animal kingdom have been placed into one of two main groups based on the presence or absence of a backbone. Animals with a backbone are called **vertebrates**, while those without a backbone are called **invertebrates**. This book is devoted to the 95 percent of all known species of animals called invertebrates. An invertebrate is any animal that does not have a backbone. The invertebrates include sponges, jellyfish, worms, insects, spiders, and starfish.

Student observers will use many scientific process skills to discover the world of invertebrates—their habits, behaviors, and natural history. The reinforcement sheets that follow the lessons contain at least one higher-level thinking question. So, student observers, put on those thinking caps and use your process skills to observe, classify, analyze, debate, design, and report. This unit contains a variety of lessons that will help you practice scientific processes as you make exciting discoveries about these incredible soft-bodied animals called invertebrates.

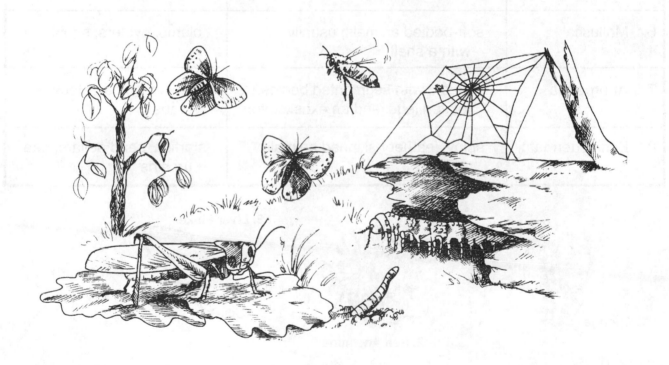

* **Teacher Note:** This book supports the National Science Education Standards and is designed to supplement your existing science curriculum. Each lesson opens with a manageable amount of text for the student to read. The succeeding pages contain exercises and illustrations that are varied and plentiful. Phonetic spellings and simple definitions for terms are also included to assist the student. The lessons may be used as a complete unit for the entire class or as supplemental material for the reluctant learner. The tone of the book is informal; a dialogue is established between the book and the student.

Name: _____ Date: _____

Invertebrates: *Eight Major Phyla*

Phyla	Description	Examples
1. Porifera	pore-bearing animals	sponges
2. Cnidarians	animals with special stinging cells	jellyfish, corals, sea anemones
3. Platyhelminthes	worms with flattened bodies	planarians, tapeworms, flukes
4. Nematoda	worms with round, tube-like bodies	pinworms, trichina worms, ascaris
5. Annelida	worms with segmented bodies	earthworms, leeches, sandworms
6. Mollusca	soft-bodied animals, usually with a shell	clams, oysters, squid
7. Arthropoda	animals with segmented bodies, jointed legs, and an exoskeleton.	insects, spiders, lobster, crabs
8. Echinodermata	spiny, leathery-skinned animals	starfish, sand dollars, sea urchins

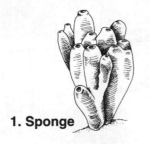

1. Sponge

2. Sea Anemone

3. Liver Fluke

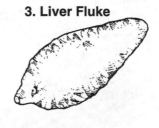

4. Ascaris

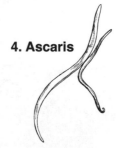

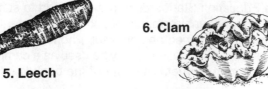

5. Leech

6. Clam

7. Crab

8. Sand Dollar

Animals: *A Special Group of Organisms*

The branch of science that deals with the study of animals is called **zoology**. There are roughly nine to ten million species of animals that inhabit the earth. Most animals inhabit the seas and oceans. A few animals live in fresh water, and even fewer live on land. Animals come in many sizes. They range from no more than a few cells to organisms weighing many tons. Scientists have determined five main traits to help identify an organism as an animal. The animal kingdom is made up of more kinds of **organisms** (living things) than the other four kingdoms. Let's take a closer look at the characteristics all animals share.

Animal Characteristics

- Animals cannot make their own food. (They eat other organisms.)
- Animals have many cells.
- Animals have eukaryotic cells. (They have a true nucleus.)
- Animals move about.
- Animals digest their food. (They must break down the food into molecules small enough for their bodies to use.)

Vertebrate or Invertebrate?

When identifying animals, scientists look to see if the animal has a backbone. If the animal has a backbone, it is called a **vertebrate**. They are the most complex and familiar animals. You are a vertebrate. If you run your hand down your back, you can feel your backbone. Your backbone is made of many small bones and cartilage called **vertebrae**. Vertebrates have an **endoskeleton**, a skeleton on the inside of the body. The endoskeleton shapes and supports the organism while protecting soft body parts.

If the animal does not have a backbone, it is called an **invertebrate**. Most animals are invertebrates; invertebrates make up 95 percent of all the known animals. Some invertebrates have an **exoskeleton**, a skeleton on the outside of the body. The exoskeleton protects and supports the soft-bodied animal. It is made of a hard, waterproof substance called **chitin**. The exoskeleton limits the growth and size of the animal. It must be **molted** (shed) in order for the animal to grow. The grasshopper must molt its exoskeleton several times in order to reach adulthood. Other invertebrates are soft-bodied animals that do not have skeletons at all.

Name: _____   Date: _____

Animals: *A Special Group of Organisms (cont.)*

Symmetry

After deciding whether the backbone is present or not, the scientist will look next at the arrangement of the animal's body parts. This is called the animal's **symmetry**. Most animals have **bilateral symmetry**. If the animal were divided lengthwise in half, would the right and left sides match? If so, the animal has bilateral symmetry. Humans have bilateral symmetry. Some animals have body parts that are arranged in a circle like the spokes of a wheel. These animals have **radial symmetry**. Jellyfish and starfish have radial symmetry. Sponges are organisms that have no definite shape. Because of their indefinite shape, they are called **asymmetrical**. The sponge is the only animal that is asymmetrical.

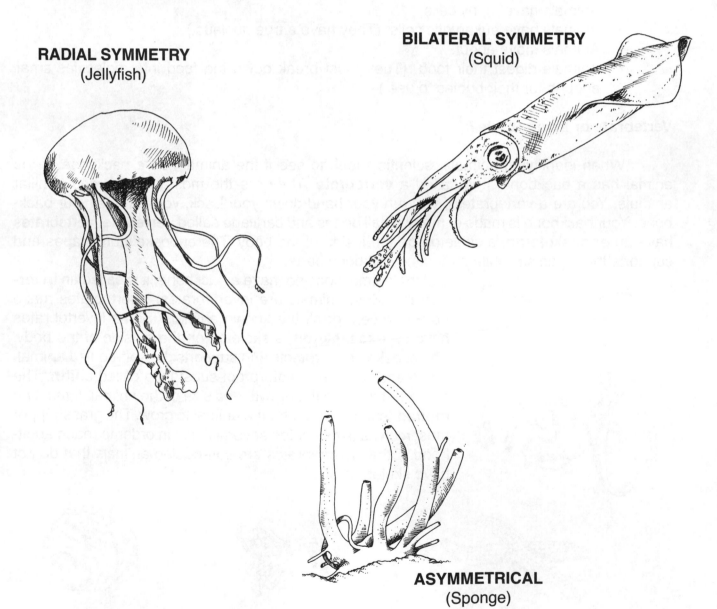

RADIAL SYMMETRY
(Jellyfish)

BILATERAL SYMMETRY
(Squid)

ASYMMETRICAL
(Sponge)

Name: _____ Date: _____

Animals: A Special Group of Organisms—*Reinforcement Activity*

To the student observer: What is the difference between a vertebrate and an invertebrate?

_____

_____

Analyze: Why do think radial symmetry is found among aquatic species rather than animals that live on land?

_____

_____

Directions: Answer the questions below based on what you have learned in this lesson.

1. What are the five characteristics all animals share in common?

    a. _____

    b. _____

    c. _____

    d. _____

    e. _____

2. What are the differences between an exoskeleton and an endoskeleton?_____

    _____

3. What must some invertebrates do in order to grow? Why? _____

    _____

    _____

4. What is chitin? _____

    _____

5. Which invertebrate has no symmetry? _____

6. After a scientist determines an organism is an animal, what does he or she look for next?

    a. _____

    b. _____

Keeping Track: *Classification of Invertebrates*

Invertebrates, like all living things, are placed into groups, which makes it easier to study and learn about them. For example, suppose you wanted to go to the store and look for a certain CD you've been wanting to buy. To make it easier for you to find the CD you want, the store organizes them according to the type of music and then in alphabetical order. In the same way, all **organisms** (living things) are organized or put into groups based on the traits they have in common. Scientists look at organisms' similarities as well as their differences, which helps them place the organisms into their proper groups. They are grouped and regrouped until every organism in the group is one of a kind. Then the group has only one species in it, and each species is given a scientific name. The name given to the organism is based on the Latin language, because Latin is the common scientific language throughout the world. In this way, scientists can keep track of the many different kinds of organisms.

Carolus Linnaeus developed a system of assigning every organism a name and of classifying each organism according to its system, size, shape, color, and method of obtaining food. This two-word naming system is called **binomial nomenclature** and was developed to help scientists avoid errors in communication. *Binomial nomenclature* means "two names." The two-word name is commonly called the organism's **scientific name**, and it is always written in italics. The scientific name is made up of the **genus** name and the **species** name. The first letter of the first word (genus name) is always capitalized, and the second word (species name) is always in lower case. An example of a scientific name is *Canis familiaris* (the dog). A specific name for every organism avoids confusion when scientists communicate because there are often too many common names for an animal, which can be misleading. For example, prairie dogs are more similar to squirrels than dogs; a starfish is not a fish, yet a seahorse is a fish.

The modern classification used today is based on a five-kingdom system. These kingdoms are *Animal, Plant, Fungi, Protista,* and *Monera.* The science of classifying and naming organisms is called **taxonomy**. To be considered an animal, the organism must have **eukaryotic cells** (cells with a nucleus), it must have many cells, and it must be able to move about. It is not able to make its own food but must eat other organisms and digest its food.

Invertebrates are **classified** or divided into eight main phyla: sponges, cnidarians, flatworms, roundworms, segmented worms, mollusks, arthropods, and echinoderms.

Name: _____ Date: _____

Classification: *Reinforcement Activity*

To the student observer: Can you explain why classification is necessary?

_____

_____

Analyze: Why can't taxonomists group organisms simply by their appearance?

_____

_____

Directions: Answer the following questions about classification.

1. What does it mean to "classify" living things? _____

    _____

2. Why do scientists classify organisms? _____

    _____

3. What is a taxonomist? _____

    _____

4. What is binomial nomenclature? _____

    _____

5. How do you write an organism's scientific name? _____

    _____

6. List the different characteristics scientists use to classify organisms.

    a. _____

    b. _____

    c. _____

    d. _____

    e. _____

7

Invertebrates: *What Is a Sponge?*

Kingdom: *Animalia*
    Phylum: *Porifera* [por IF er uh], means "pore-bearer"

Characteristics

In the past, people thought sponges were plants because they did not move from place to place like most animals do. All sponges are invertebrates that live in water. They are mostly **marine** (live in salt water), but some do live in fresh water. These special underwater invertebrates are the simplest of all the animals. They do not have heads, arms, legs, or any internal organs. Sponges grow in many different colors, sizes, and shapes. They are usually classified as **asymmetrical** (lacking symmetry or likeness of body parts). The adult sponge does not move about. Sponges attach themselves to plants or rocks on the ocean floor. The adult sponge is **sessile** (remains in one place for the rest of its life). It's no wonder that early scientists classified sponges as plants!

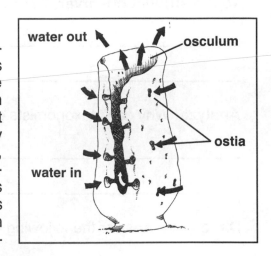

Obtaining Food

Scientists observed the sponge and discovered that it obtains its food the same way other animals do. It eats other living creatures to get the nourishment it needs to live. A sponge filters its food from the water as it is pulled in through **pores**, or holes, called **ostia** on the sides of its body. Bacteria, algae, and protozoa are filtered out of the water as it flows through the sponge to be used as food. Organisms that obtain food this way are called **filter-feeders**.

Wandering cells

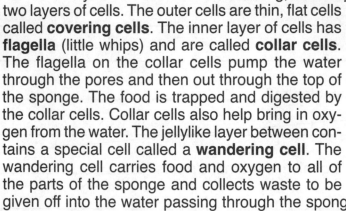

As you can see from the drawing, the body of a sponge is made up of two layers of cells. The outer cells are thin, flat cells called **covering cells**. The inner layer of cells has **flagella** (little whips) and are called **collar cells**. The flagella on the collar cells pump the water through the pores and then out through the top of the sponge. The food is trapped and digested by the collar cells. Collar cells also help bring in oxygen from the water. The jellylike layer between contains a special cell called a **wandering cell**. The wandering cell carries food and oxygen to all of the parts of the sponge and collects waste to be given off into the water passing through the sponge. The jellylike middle also contains small needlelike support structures called **spicules**. They link together to form a simple skeleton that supports and shapes the body of a sponge. You might compare the body of a sponge to an empty sack. The sponge is hollow on the inside and has a large opening called an **osculum** at the top.

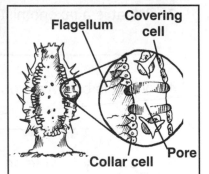

Spicules

Reproduction

Sponges can reproduce **sexually** (two parents producing offspring) or **asexually** (one parent producing offspring). When the sponge reproduces asexually, it forms an outgrowth called a **bud** from the parent sponge. This form of asexual reproduction is called **budding**. When the young bud is fully developed, it breaks off from the parent sponge. Sponges can also reproduce asexually by **regeneration**. If the sponge is cut into pieces and then returned to the ocean, each piece begins to replace or grow back its missing body parts. If the sponge is cut into three pieces, you have three sponges.

Name: _____ Date: _____

What Is a Sponge?: *Reinforcement Activity: Crossword Puzzle*

To the student observer: Why did scientists reclassify the sponge? _____

_____

Analyze: In your opinion, why do you believe scientists consider sponges to be the simplest animals?

_____

_____

Directions: Use what you learned about sponges to complete the following crossword puzzle.

ACROSS

8. Sponges are _____.
9. Water enters the sponge here.
10. Sponges have only _____ cell layers.
11. Most sponges live in the _____.
12. Sponges obtain food by _____.
14. To replace missing parts
17. These pump water through the sponge.

DOWN

1. An asexual form of reproduction
2. Once considered a _____; the sponge is now classified as an animal.

3. _____ cells carry food and oxygen.
4. Ocean living
5. Lack of symmetry
6. Means "pore-bearer"
7. Holes
11. Support the sponge
12. Little whips
13. Remains in one place for life
15. Water leaves the sponge here.
16. A sponge compares to an empty _____.

Invertebrates: *What Is a Cnidarian?*

Kingdom: *Animalia*
   Phylum: *Cnidaria* [ni DER ee uh] means "stinging cells."

Student observers, have you ever seen a jellyfish? If you have, then you have seen a **cnidarian**. The cnidarians include some of the most beautiful animals. They include jellyfish, hydras, sea anemones, and corals. Today, we are going to study these amazing aquatic animals. Most cnidarians live in **marine** (salt) water, but a few, such as the hydra, live in fresh water. These simple, radially symmetrical animals are flower-like and in some ways resemble plants. **Radial symmetry** means that the body radiates out in all directions from the center like the spokes of a wheel. *Cnidaria* is Latin for "stinging cells."

Complexity and Structure

These animals find themselves up one step of the ladder of complexity from the sponges. They are still very simple animals, but they are more complex than the sponge. They have **two cell layers** that are organized into **tissue**. Cnidarians have digestive, muscle, nerve, and sensory tissue. The cnidarian body is a hollow sack with only one body opening (a mouth). It is surrounded by rope-like pieces of tissue called **tentacles** (arms). These tentacles may contain **cnidocytes** (stinging cells), which are used to capture food. These cells contain poison arrows connected to threads called **nematocysts**. When a small fish touches the tentacle, the arrow shoots out to paralyze the prey. The tentacle then brings the victim to the mouth and into a simple digestive cavity. After the prey is digested inside the hollow sack, the food passes into the body cells, and the waste must go back out the mouth.

Body Forms

The cnidarian has two body forms or shapes as shown below. Some have an umbrella shape where the mouth and tentacles hang down. This body plan is called **Medusa** (muh DOO suh). The Medusa form can float on the surface of water and swim about. Other cnidarians, such as the corals, hydras, and sea anemones, have a **polyp** form. A polyp does not usually move about; its tube-shaped body is attached to the bottom of the ocean, with the mouth and tentacles pointing upward.

Most jellyfish live as individuals. Some polyps tend to live in colonies or groups as the corals do. The corals secrete a calcium carbonate shelter around their bodies. In time, the shelters join together with neighboring corals to form coral reefs.

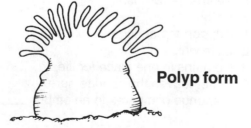

Polyp form

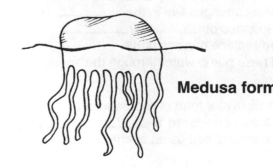

Medusa form

10

Name: _____ Date: _____

What Is a Cnidarian?: *Reinforcement Activity*

To the student observer: Do you know which animals are cnidarians? _____
_____

Analyze: How is a jellyfish more complex than a sponge? _____
_____
_____

Directions: Use what you have learned about cnidarians to answer the following questions.

1. How did cnidarians get their name? _____
   _____

2. How would a jellyfish catch a fish? _____
   _____
   _____

3. How do the tentacles of a jellyfish differ from a sea anemone? How is the difference an advantage for each animal?
   _____
   _____
   _____
   _____
   _____

4. What types of tissue do cnidarians have? _____
   _____

Directions: Write the term that best completes each sentence in the space provided.

5. Cnidarians have long arm-like tissue called _____.

6. The body form of a jellyfish is called _____.

7. The body form of a hydra is called _____.

8. The tentacles may have stinging cells called _____.

9. Cnidarians use their tentacles to capture _____.

10. Cnidarians have _____ symmetry.

Worm World: *What Is a Flatworm?*

Kingdom: *Animalia*
    Phylum: *Platyhelminthes* [plat ee hel MIN theez] means "flat and wide worms."

Student observers, what kind of animal do you think of when you hear the word *worm*? The first thing that most likely comes to mind is an earthworm. We usually see earthworms when we dig in the dirt or go fishing, or they may be crawling on the sidewalk after a rain. However, there are many kinds of worms. Worms are **classified** (grouped) into three different phyla: **flatworms**, **roundworms**, and **segmented worms**.

All worms are invertebrates with soft bodies and bilateral symmetry. **Bilateral symmetry** means that the worm has matching right and left sides (mirror images) when you divide it in half lengthwise. They have three cell layers—the **ectoderm** [EK tuh durm] or outer layer, the **mesoderm** [MES uh durm] or middle layer, and the **endoderm** [EN duh durm] or inner layer. The three tissue layers are organized into organs and organ systems. They have identifiable front and rear ends as well as tops and bottoms. They live in many different environments. Some are free-living and do not require a host organism to obtain food and a place to live. Others are parasitic and do require a host organism in order to live. In this lesson, you will learn about the flatworms.

Types of Flatworms—Planarians

Flatworms have flattened bodies, and they are the simplest worms. They are members of the phylum *Platyhelminthes* and include three groups. One group lives in ponds and streams; they are free-living and the most common flatworms, the **planarians** [pluh NER ee uhns]. Planarians do not depend on another organism or host in order to survive. The planarian is one step up on the ladder of complexity from the cnidarians. They have specialized organs that are organized into simple systems. Like the cnidarians, they too have only one body opening for food to come in and for waste to leave. Planarians are more advanced, however, in that they have nerve organs called **eyespots** on their triangle-shaped heads for detecting and reacting to light. The eyespots are located on the **anterior** (front end). They have bilateral symmetry that allows them to move forward. Their bodies are covered with tiny hairs called **cilia**. The cilia move the worm along in a **mucus** (a slimy substance) track secreted by the underside of the planarian. Planarians eat small organisms and the dead bodies of larger organisms. They live in fresh water or moist habitats under rocks or on plants. Planarians reproduce **asexually** (one parent produces offspring) by simply dividing in two. They can also regenerate. Regeneration is the ability to regrow lost or damaged parts. A planarian can be cut in two, and the two halves will each grow into a new worm.

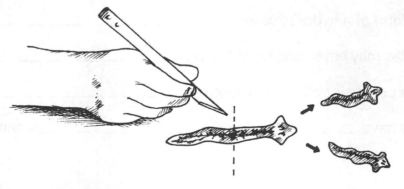

Worm World: *Other Flatworms*

The other two groups of flatworms are **parasites** that require a host organism in order to live. They feed on and usually cause harm to the host. The tapeworm and fluke are both parasites. They have special body parts, **hooks and suckers**, that help them live inside another organism. Tapeworms do not have a mouth or digestive system. The tapeworm lives in the intestine of almost every kind of animal, including man. In the intestine, they absorb food that is already digested by the host. Tapeworms can grow to several meters in length. The fluke is a broad, flat, parasitic worm. One type of fluke lives in the liver of humans.

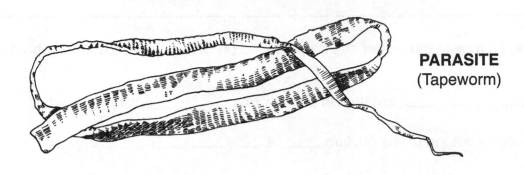

PARASITE
(Tapeworm)

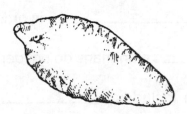

PARASITE
(Liver fluke)

FREE-LIVING
(Planarian)

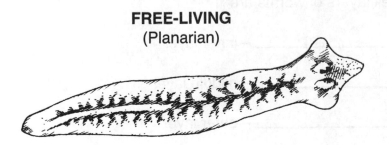

Name: _____   Date: _____

What Is a Flatworm?: *Reinforcement Activity*

To the student observer: Do you know what a flatworm is? _____

_____

_____

Analyze: How are flatworms more complex than cnidarians? _____

_____

_____

Directions: Complete the sentences below based on what you have learned about flatworms.

1. _____ are the simplest worms.

2. Flatworms belong to the phylum _____.

3. The _____ is a flatworm parasite found in the intestine of almost every

   kind of animal.

4. Parasites require a _____ in order to live.

5. The _____ planarians do not depend on other organisms for survival.

6. The flatworm phylum includes _____, _____, and

   _____.

7. The planarians can _____ damaged parts.

8. The three cell layers of worms are:

   a. _____ – inner layer

   b. _____ – middle layer

   c. _____ – outer layer

Worm World: *What Is a Roundworm?*

Kingdom: *Animalia*
    Phylum: *Nematoda* [nee muh TOH duh] means "thread-like."

Do you own a dog? If you do, you've had to get medicine from your veterinarian to protect your dog from roundworms. Roundworms are one of the most successful groups of animals. They live in a wide range of habitats, in all types of water and soil. Most are free-living, but some species are parasites of animals and plants. It is estimated that there are more than a half-million species of these **nematodes**. Roundworms belong to the phylum nematoda, which includes a more complex group of worms. They have a mouth for obtaining food and an anus for getting rid of waste. This continuous digestive

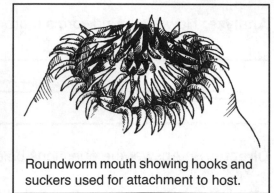

Roundworm mouth showing hooks and suckers used for attachment to host.

system makes them more complex than the flatworms. Like flatworms, they have muscle, nerve, excretory, and reproductive organs that form simple systems. They have a very tough **cuticle** (waxy covering) that little can penetrate. This is one reason they can survive as parasites inside animals and plants.

Types of Roundworms

There are about 50 species of parasitic roundworms. The **hookworm** is a roundworm parasite of humans. Shoes should always be worn when outdoors, as hookworm can be acquired by walking barefoot over dirt or through fields. Hookworm eggs hatch in warm, moist soil. **Ascaris** [AS kuh ris], another roundworm parasite, lives in the intestines of pigs, horses, and humans. Eggs can enter the host's body through contaminated food or water. The eggs travel to the intestines where they mature and mate; if left untreated, the worms can block the intestines, causing death.

The **heartworm**, a parasitic worm in dogs, is transmitted to your dog through a mosquito bite. The heartworms move to the heart where they grow and reproduce. If left untreated, the heartworms will eventually block the valves of the heart. You can give your dog medicine once a month to prevent heartworms. The **trichina** worm causes the disease trichinosis. Humans become infected when they eat rare, undercooked pork that has trichinella cysts. A **cyst** is a young worm with a protective covering. Trichinosis may result in death, so pork must always be cooked thoroughly.

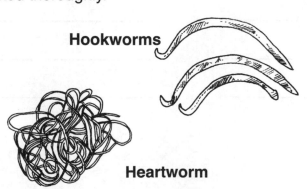

Hookworms

Heartworm

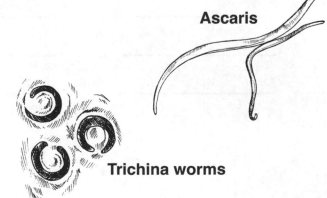

Ascaris

Trichina worms

Name: _____ Date: _____

What Is a Roundworm?: *Reinforcement Activity*

To the student observer: How can you prevent getting hookworms? _____

_____

Analyze: How are roundworms more advanced than the flatworms? _____

_____

_____

_____

Directions: Answer the questions below based on what you have learned about roundworms.

1. Roundworms belong to the phylum _____.

2. Most roundworms are _____, but some are _____.

3. Roundworms have four types of organs: _____, _____,

   _____, and _____.

4. Roundworms are so successful because they have a tough, waxy covering called the

   _____.

5. Roundworms have a _____ or complete digestive system.

Directions: Fill in the word associated with the correct parasite.

rare   soil   cysts   pork   dog   feet   intestines   monthly   mosquito

Hookworm	Heartworm	Trichina Worm
_____	_____	_____
_____	_____	_____
_____	_____	_____

Worm World: *What Is a Segmented Worm?*

Kingdom: *Animalia*
   Phylum: *Annelida* [an nuh LEE duh] means "ringed."

The most complex worms are the **segmented worms**, also called *annelids*. These worms have bodies with many segments, "ring-like sections," running from head to tail. There are approximately 9,000 species of annelids. Most live in the ocean, but some live in fresh water. The best-known segmented worm is the **earthworm**, which lives in soil. Annelids also include **bristle worms**, **marine worms**, and **leeches**. The annelids are up one more step of the ladder of complexity. They are more advanced than the roundworms and all the other phyla below them because they have a **coelom** [SEE lom]. A coelom is a liquid-filled space or body cavity that holds the internal organs. On the outside of their bodies they have **setae** or bristle-like structures they use to burrow into the soil.

Types of Segmented Worms—Earthworms

Earthworms are the most advanced worms. They burrow in soil and live in moist areas. Earthworms have complex systems. They have blood vessels that carry food to all the cells. Because their blood remains inside **vessels** (a system of tubes), they have a closed circulatory system. If the blood moves through open spaces in an animal's body and does not flow through tubes, it has an open circulatory system. Earthworms also have a more advanced digestive system. They have a **crop** where the food is stored and a **gizzard** that grinds the food. The food is then digested in the intestines. Earthworms have a nervous system; nerves run along the body connecting to a simple brain at the **anterior** (front end). They have an excretory system of tubes that removes liquid waste from each segment. Earthworms lack a respiratory system, however. They exchange gases by diffusion through their moist skin. Earthworms respond to light, temperature, and moisture. Earthworms tunnel through the earth and loosen the soil, which lets air reach the plant roots, and their waste material adds nutrients to the soil. They are often called the "farmer's friend."

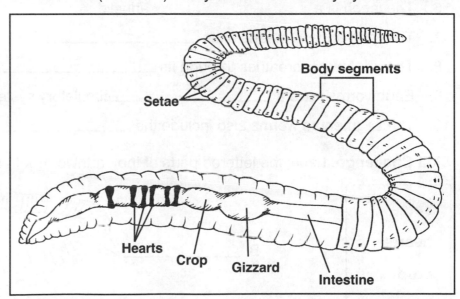

Leeches

Have you ever been swimming in a pond, lake, or river? If so, you may have had to remove a leech from your body. The leech is a parasitic, segmented worm and lives on the surface of other animals. Leeches use their suckers to attach themselves and feed on the blood of the host animal. At one time, leeches were used to suck "bad blood" from sick people; however, this was not a good practice. Today, leeches are used in microsurgery to keep blood flowing to reattached body parts. The leech secretes a chemical in its saliva that keeps the blood flowing and prevents it from clotting. As a result, the reattached tissue remains healthy.

Name: _____ Date: _____

What Is a Segmented Worm?: *Reinforcement Activity*

To the student observer: Can you describe a segmented worm? _____
_____

Analyze: Why are earthworms called the farmer's friend? _____
_____
_____

Directions: Use the word bank to complete the sentences below.

bristle worms	advanced	leeches	parasitic	closed
skin	annelida	setae	rings	coelom

1. Segmented worms are the most _____ worms.

2. Segmented worms belong to the _____ phylum.

3. The _____ is a liquid-filled space that holds the internal organs.

4. At one time, doctors used _____ to suck "bad blood" from their patients.

5. Segmented worms use _____ for movement.

6. The leech is a _____ annelid.

7. The term annelid means "little _____."

8. The earthworm breathes through its _____.

9. Earthworms have a _____ circulatory system.

10. The segmented worms also include the _____.

Skill Challenge: Label the lettered parts of the earthworm with the terms in the word bank.

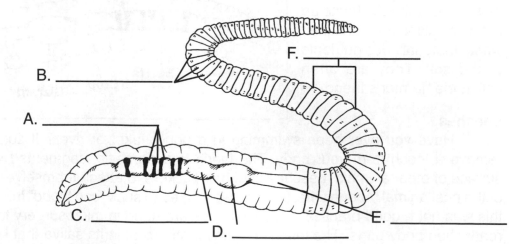

setae

hearts

crop

gizzard

intestine

segments

B. _____

A. _____

C. _____

D. _____

F. _____

E. _____

Watching Worms Squirm: *Constructing a Wormery*

Observers, making a wormery to watch earthworms move can be fun. Earthworms live just beneath the surface of the soil. As they tunnel through the earth using their setae (bristles), they loosen the soil. The earthworm is often called the farmer's friend. The tunnels let air reach the plant roots, and the waste material they leave behind adds nutrients to the soil. Watch these useful creatures work as they stretch and pull themselves through the soil.

Materials:
earthworms (miniature plows)
two plastic bottles—one large bottle and one small bottle
various soil types: sand, earth, peat
powdered chalk

Procedure:
1. Cut the tops off of each plastic bottle. Place the small bottle inside the larger bottle.
2. Put a layer of one soil type around the outside of the small bottle.
3. Add some powdered chalk on top of the first layer. (The chalk helps you to see the tunnels more easily.)
4. Alternate layers of various soil types and add some chalk on top of each new layer. Leave a space of 2.5 cm (1″) at the top
5. Add a layer of dead leaves or grass clippings and moisten the soil with water. Be careful not to get the soil too wet.
6. Add a few large earthworms to the space at the top of the wormery.
7. Cover the wormery with a towel. Worms avoid light. Wait two days before you lift the towel to take a peek. Always keep the wormery covered when you are not making observations. Don't forget to water the soil lightly. (Keep the soil moist.)
8. Have fun watching the worms make their tunnels!

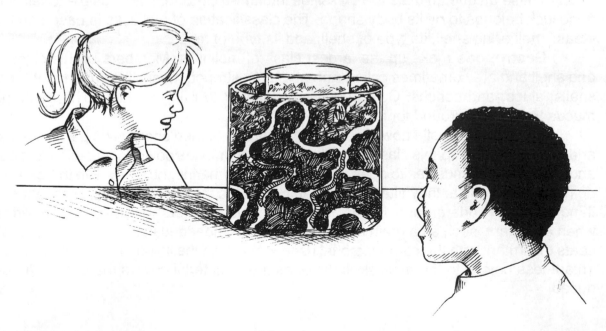

Invertebrates: *What Is a Mollusk?*

Kingdom: *Animalia*
    Phylum: *Mollusca* [mo LUSK uh] means "soft-bodied."

The phylum mollusca is made up of soft-bodied invertebrates that usually have a shell. **Mollusks** may appear to be very different, but they are all structurally similar. They are found living on land and in fresh and salt water. They include animals such as clams, oysters, snails, slugs, octopus, and squid. Have you ever eaten a clam? If you have, you know that most of the body is soft and slimy.

Body Plan

    Mollusks have a soft body, usually covered by a hard shell. The soft body is covered and protected by a **mantle**. The mantle, a thin membrane, secretes the shell for many mollusks. The mollusk has three body parts: head, foot, and a visceral mass. The **head** contains the brain and sensory organs, the **foot** is the muscular part of the body and may be divided into parts (i.e., the octopus). The **visceral mass** area is the space in which the body parts are located.

    Most mollusks have well-developed organs that form various systems. They have an open circulatory system. The blood is not always inside the blood vessels the way a human's blood is—it fills open spaces in the body and bathes the organs. Mollusks also have a digestive system, reproductive system, and nervous system. The octopus and squid have a jet-action water vascular system they use for swimming. The water is forced out through a tube-like structure near the head, which sends the mollusks quickly in the opposite direction. Another special structure found in some mollusks, such as the snail, is the **radula** [RAJ oo luh]. The radula is a rough, tongue-like organ that is used to scrape algae off of rocks. Some people even use snails to clean the glass sides of their aquariums.

Classifying Mollusks

    These unique animals are classified into three classes. It is possible to tell which group a mollusk belongs to by its body shape. The classification of mollusks is based on these three ideas: shell or no shell, its type of shell, and its type of foot.

    Gastropods make up the largest class of mollusks. Members of this class have only one shell and are sometimes called **univalves**. Gastropod means "stomach foot" and includes snails, slugs, and conchs. Gastropods are adapted to living on land. The gastropod lays a mucus trail on the ground for its foot to glide over.

    Bivalves are well-known mollusks that have a hinged shell in two parts. Clams, oysters, and scallops make up this class of mollusks. The clam uses powerful muscles to close its shell and relaxes these muscles to open its shell. Most are marine, but a few live in fresh water. They do not have a radula; they filter-feed organic particles through their gills. Most attach to something or burrow underground. Many mollusks—not just oysters—make pearls. Pearls are made when an irritant, such as a grain of sand, becomes embedded in the mantle. The mollusk then coats the irritant with the same material used to produce the lining of its shell, which makes the irritant less painful to the mollusk. In time, as more material covers the irritant, a pearl is produced.

Invertebrates: *What Is a Mollusk? (cont.)*

The **cephalopods** live in the ocean and are adapted for swimming. They are the most specialized and complex members of the mollusca phylum. Cephalopods, which means "head-footed," have a large well-developed head and a foot, which is divided into many arms. The feet, or arms of these amazing creatures are connected to their heads, not their bodies. The body is in front of the head. These mollusks usually do not have an external shell and include the octopus, squid, cuttlefish, and nautilus. However, the chambered nautilus is an exception; they are the only member of the cephalopods that has a heavy external shell. To swim or float, they have a unique adaptation that allows them to fill their shell with a gas. Although they appear to be very different from the other mollusks, they are similar. They have a mantle, a mantle cavity, a radula, and a similar digestive tract. Cephalopods have a strong beak that is used for biting into prey. The octopus and squid have arms with disc-shaped suckers used for gripping their prey. They can squeeze into a space one-tenth the size of their body. Have you ever wondered what the difference is between an octopus and a squid? An octopus has eight arms and a squid has ten (two are longer than the other eight). The blue-ringed octopus is the most toxic cephalopod; a bite is nearly always fatal to humans.

Name: _____ Date: _____

What Is a Mollusk?: *Reinforcement Activity*

Directions: Label the mollusk with the correct class name: **bivalve, cephalopod, gastropod**.

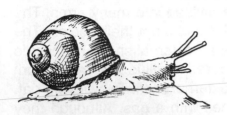  

A. _____ B. _____ C. _____

Directions: Complete the sentences below with the correct word from the word bank.

octopus	**soft-bodied**	**pearl**	**open**	**shell**	**radula**
mantle	**water vascular**				

1. All mollusks are _____ invertebrates.

2. The bodies of most mollusks are covered by a _____.

3. Mollusks have an _____ circulatory system.

4. The cephalopods have a _____ system for swimming.

5. The gastropods have a _____ or tongue-like organ.

6. Sometimes a mollusk will coat an irritant with a substance to make a _____.

7. The _____ secretes the shell for many mollusks.

8. The _____ is the most complex mollusk.

Skill Challenge: Place an "x" in the correct column or columns.

Characteristics	Gastropod	Bivalve	Cephalopod
a. one shell			
b. two-part shell			
c. arms with suckers			
d. soft, fleshy body			
e. three body parts			
f. well-developed head			
g. open circulatory system			
h. moves by jet-action			
i. no shell			
j. "housekeeper" for fish			

Name: _____ Date: _____

Research: *Mollusk Project*

Mollusks are soft-bodied animals without a backbone. Most of them have shells. Three of the most common classes are **gastropods**, **bivalves**, and **cephalopods**.

To the student observer: Draw a card from your teacher's grab bag. The cards are equally divided between the three common classes of mollusks. Based on the luck of the draw, you will choose an appropriate species to research. Pick one that interests you. You will need to gather information about your mollusk. Your research must include at least two resources. Follow your teacher's directions for the format and length of the presentation.

General list for grab bag: (Teacher may add mollusks to this list.)
Bivalves: oyster, clam, scallop, mussel, cockle, ark, angel wing, jewel box
Gastropods: land snail, abalone, conch, slug, bonnet, moon snail, murex, whelk
Cephalopods: squid, octopus, nautilus, cuttlefish

Mollusk I will research:	Class: _____
	Name of mollusk: _____
	Common and scientific names
Research Data	
Size:	
Habitat:	
Description:	

Name: _____ Date: _____

Research: *Mollusk Project (cont.)*

Behavior:

Uses for my mollusk:

Two additional facts I've learned about my mollusk:

A picture of my mollusk: (Use a photocopy or draw your own.)

Name: _____ Date: _____

Invertebrates: *What Is an Arthropod?*

Kingdom: *Animalia*
  Phylum: *Arthropoda* [AHR thruh pahd uh], means "jointed foot."

Arthropods make up the largest **phylum** (group) of animals. Arthropods are adapted to live in almost every environment. Scientists believe there are over one million species.

Arthropod Features
    Arthropods are animals that have **jointed appendages**. Appendages are structures that grow from the body. Your arms and legs are appendages. The appendages of arthropods include jointed legs, claws, pincers, and antennae. All arthropods have **segmented bodies** with a hard covering called an **exoskeleton**. The segments of some arthropods are fused together to form two or three body regions. The three body regions are the **head**, **thorax**, and **abdomen**. The exoskeleton is an external skeleton that covers and protects the body. It is made of a tough material called **chitin**. The chitin is coated with a waxy substance that makes the exoskeleton waterproof and prevents dehydration by keeping moisture in the animal's body. The exoskeleton doesn't grow with the animal as a human's skeleton does. It must be shed as the arthropod becomes too large. The old skeleton is replaced with a new one in a process called **molting**. The new exoskeleton is soft and takes some time to harden. The arthropod is not well-protected from predators during this time. Most arthropods undergo four to seven molts before reaching adult size.
    Arthropods are divided into several classes, the largest of which is **insecta**. There are more insects than any other group of invertebrates. Insects include flies, moths, grasshoppers, mosquitoes, ants, bees, and many others. In addition to insects, the arthropods also include arachnids [uh RAK nids], crustaceans [krus TAY shuns], and myriapods [MIR ee uh pahds]. **Arachnids** include spiders, mites, ticks, and scorpions. **Crustaceans** include lobsters, shrimp, crabs, and crayfish. **Myriapods** include centipedes and millipedes.

Name: _____ Date: _____

What Is an Arthropod? *Reinforcement Activity*

To the student observer: Why do you think arthropods outnumber all of the other phyla of invertebrates?

_____

_____

Analyze: Why can't we study arthropods at the phylum level? _____

_____

Directions: Use what you have learned about arthropods to answer the following questions.

1. What are appendages? _____

_____

2. What are the three main characteristics of an arthropod?

   a. _____

   b. _____

   c. _____

3. What are the three body regions of most arthropods?

   a. _____

   b. _____

   c. _____

4. Describe the exoskeleton. What is it made of? _____

_____

5. Explain molting. _____

_____

6. Why must arthropods molt? _____

_____

7. What is the largest class of arthropods? _____

_____

8. Besides insecta, what are the three other classes of arthropods?

   a. _____

   b. _____

   c. _____

Arthropods: *What Is an Insect?*

Kingdom: *Animalia*
   Phylum: *Arthropoda*
      Class: *Insecta*

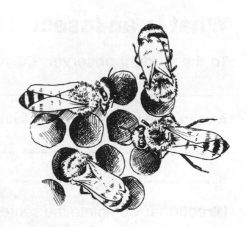

Insects are remarkably successful creatures, and are the largest class of arthropods. Insects have become adapted to every environment; they live on land, in the air, and in water. They can be found in scorching or freezing habitats. They have segmented bodies, jointed legs, and hard, protective **exoskeletons** (skeletons on the outside). Insects are different from other arthropods because they have six jointed legs, wings to help them escape from predators and hunt for food, and three body regions. They have a **head**, a **thorax**, and an **abdomen**. Insects have **spiracles**, openings or air tubes for breathing. The air moves in and out through the spiracles on their abdomen or thorax. Insects use a structure under their wings called a **tympanum** for hearing. They have sensory organs called **antennae** that detect air movement, vibrations, and smells. Insects also have three simple eyes and two compound eyes. **Simple eyes** detect light and dark. **Compound eyes** are made up of many lenses that allow the insect to detect color and movement in all directions at once. An insect has specialized mouth parts unique for eating plant material. They have **mandibles** for chewing, a **maxilla** to push or suck food into the mouth, and a **labium** that acts as a lower lip to hold food. The grasshopper makes a good model for the study of insect parts. Observe the parts of the grasshopper below.

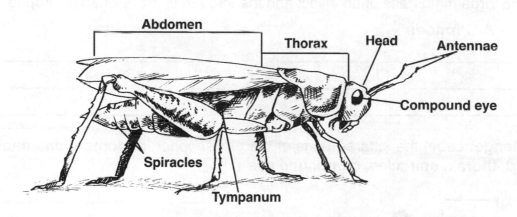

Most insects live alone; however, some do live in colonies. Insects that live in colonies are called **social animals**. Ants and bees are examples of social insects. Honeybees live in a hive. The beehive is made up of three kinds of bees: the queen, the drone, and the worker. Each bee has its own job to do within the social unit. The **queen bee** is busy laying eggs. The job of the **drone** is to fertilize the eggs. The **worker bee** stays busy gathering honey and protecting the hive.

Name: _____ Date: _____

What Is an Insect?: *Reinforcement Activity*

To the student observer: Do you know to which class of arthropods a butterfly belongs?

_____

Analyze: In your opinion, is living within a colony an advantage for some animals? Why?

_____

_____

Directions: Complete the sentences below based on what you have learned about insects.

1. Insects have openings called _____ for breathing.
2. Insects use a _____ for hearing.
3. Insects have two _____ eyes made up of many lenses.

Directions: Answer the following questions about insects.

4. What are insects who live together in colonies called? _____
5. What are the three kinds of bees within a colony called? Explain each bee's job.

   a. _____

   b. _____

   c. _____

6. List the three main traits of an insect and the three main traits of an arthropod.

Arthropods	**Insects**
a. _____	a. _____
b. _____	b. _____
c. _____	c. _____

Skill Challenge: Label the lettered parts of the grasshopper: **abdomen, antennae, tympanum, head, thorax, spiracles, compound eye**

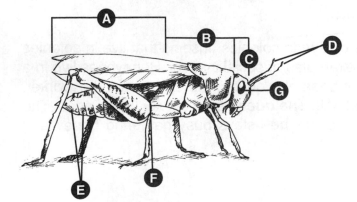

A. _____

B. _____

C. _____

D. _____

E. _____

F. _____

G. _____

Name: _____ Date: _____

Arthropods: *How Do Insects Develop?*

All insects reproduce sexually. Females lay thousands of eggs, but only a few of the eggs develop into adults. They overproduce eggs so each insect species will continue.

Metamorphosis

Metamorphosis means the change of body form and appearance. All insects hatch from eggs. Most complex insect eggs hatch to produce a larva that is very different from the adult in both form and appearance. Other insect eggs hatch to produce a miniature form of the adult. These changes that an insect goes through in becoming an adult are called metamorphosis. There are two kinds of metamorphosis—complete and incomplete.

Complete Metamorphosis

Have you ever seen a butterfly flying about the flowers? It's difficult to believe that just a short time before, it was a caterpillar crawling along the ground. The caterpillar changes form completely to become a butterfly. Insects such as moths, beetles, bees, and flies also develop by **complete metamorphosis**. These insects go through four states: egg, larva [LAHR vuh], pupa [PYOU puh], and adult. The egg hatches into a **larva**; the larva is the worm-like stage. A **caterpillar** is the larva stage of a butterfly or moth. The larva grows quickly and enters the next stage (a resting stage) called **pupa**. During the pupa state, the insects spins a **cocoon** [kuh KOON] around itself; it does not eat during this time and goes through many changes. While inside the pupa (cocoon), the whole body is reorganized, and a winged adult emerges as the cocoon opens.

Incomplete Metamorphosis

Grasshoppers, lice, and crickets develop by incomplete metamorphosis. During **incomplete metamorphosis**, the young stage resembles the adult stage. There are only three stages in incomplete metamorphosis: egg, nymph [nimf], and adult. The egg hatches into a **nymph**, which looks like the adult, only smaller. The nymph goes through a gradual transformation as it sheds its **exoskeleton** (outside skeleton) several times as it matures. This process is called **molting**.

COMPLETE METAMORPHOSIS

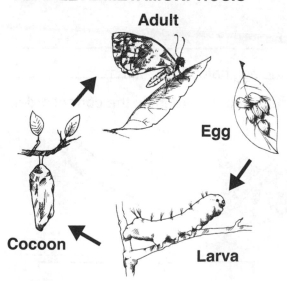

INCOMPLETE METAMORPHOSIS

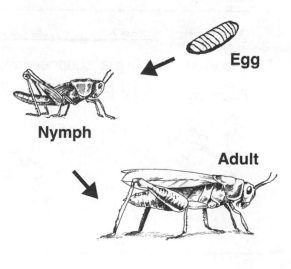

Name: _____ Date: _____

How Do Insects Develop?: *Reinforcement Activity*

To the student observer: Have you ever seen any insects going through metamorphosis? Can you name the insects?

_____

_____

Analyze: What is the main difference between the two types of life cycles that insects go through?

_____

_____

Directions: Answer the following questions about insect life cycles.

1. What is metamorphosis? _____

   _____

2. What are the two kinds of metamorphosis?

   a. _____ b. _____

3. The stages a butterfly goes through during insect development are _____,

   _____, _____., and _____.

   What is this called? _____

4. What is the caterpillar stage of insect development called? _____

5. What happens during the pupa stage? _____

   _____

6. The stages a grasshopper goes through in becoming an adult are _____,

   _____, _____.

   What is this called? _____

7. Into what stage in grasshopper development does the egg hatch? _____

8. Apply your knowledge by placing the stages of butterfly development in the correct order.

  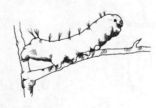

A. _____   B. _____   C. _____   D. _____

     30

Name: _____ Date: _____

Arthropods: *Other Classes of Arthropods*

Insects may be the largest group, but they aren't the only arthropods. There are several other classes of arthropods: arachnids, crustaceans, centipedes, and millipedes.

Arachnids

Arachnids are arthropods with two body regions. The head and chest region are fused into a region called the **cephalothorax**. The other region is the **abdomen**. They have four pairs of legs (8) but no antennae. Arachnids have poison glands, stingers, or fangs. They exchange oxygen and carbon dioxide through structures called **book lungs**. The spiracles on the abdomen let oxygen and carbon dioxide move into and out of the book lungs. Spiders use their fangs to inject a poison into their prey. The poison paralyzes the prey, and the spider releases an enzyme that turns the prey into a liquid. The spider then sucks up the liquid.

The spider is only one example of an arachnid. Arachnids include scorpions, mites, and ticks. Mites and ticks are the parasitic arachnids. A parasite is an animal that obtains food from a host.

Crustaceans

Crustaceans are many people's favorite arthropods. Do you like shrimp, crab, or lobster? These are members of class crustacea. Crustaceans are a source of food for many animals, including man. Crustaceans must molt their exoskeleton in order to grow. Crustaceans have one or two antennae, five pairs of legs, and most live in water. The front legs are claws for catching prey. Crustaceans use gills on the base of each leg for breathing. An amazing adaptation of crustaceans is their ability to **regenerate** (regrow) a lost appendage. If they lose a claw, they simply grow a new one.

Chilopods (Centipedes) and Diplopods (Millipedes)

The **myriapod** class of arthropods includes **chilopods (centipedes) and diplopods (millipedes)**, which have bodies divided into many sections, an exoskeleton, jointed legs, antennae, and simple eyes. The **centipede** has one pair of legs per body segment, a poison claw, and it feeds on prey. It has a flattened body and is known as the hundred-legged worm. However, adult centipedes have only fifteen pairs of legs, not one hundred. **Millipedes** have two pairs of legs per segment, move slower than centipedes, and feed on plants. They are gray to brown in color. Millipedes are known as the thousand-legged worms, but the adults actually have only 30 pairs of legs.

Name: _____ Date: _____

Other Classes of Arthropods: *Reinforcement Activity*

To the student observer: Explain how a spider obtains its food. _____

_____

_____

_____

Analyze: Can you compare and contrast the centipede and millipede? _____

_____

_____

_____

Directions: Complete the sentences based on what you have learned about the other classes of arthropods.

1. Arthropods make up the _____ animal group.

2. Spiders use structures called _____ lungs to breathe.

3. Spiders belong to a group called _____.

4. Arachnids have _____ legs and no antennae.

5. Arachnids include _____, _____, _____,

    and _____.

6. _____ are a food source for many animals, including man.

7. Crustaceans include _____, _____, and

    _____.

8. Arthropods must _____ in order to grow.

9. Crustaceans can _____ their claws.

10. The two divisions of worm-like arthropods are the _____ and the

    _____.

Name: _____ Date: _____

Name That Arthropod: *Reinforcement Activity*

To the student observer: Can you properly classify the arthropods below? Write the name of the arthropod class for each animal below using the words in the word bank.

Insect   Arachnid   Crustacean   Diplopod   Chilopod

A. _____   B. _____   C. _____

8 legs, no antennae, 2 body regions

8 legs, no antennae, 2 body regions

6 legs, antennae, 3 body regions

D. _____   E. _____   F. _____

3 body regions, wings, 6 legs, antennae

8 legs, no antennae, 2 body regions

10 legs, front claws, first pair

G. _____   H. _____   I. _____

2 pairs of legs per body segment, rounded body

10 appendages— front claws, antennae

1 pair of legs per segment, a poison claw; more flattened body than G

Name: _____ Date: _____

Invertebrates: *What Is an Echinoderm?*

Kingdom: *Animalia*
    Phylum: *Echinodermata* [Ee KINE o der MAT a] means "spiny-skinned."

    The phylum echinodermata includes the starfish, sea urchin, sea cucumber, brittle star, and sand dollar. All echinoderms live on the ocean bottom. Echinodermata means "spiny-skinned." The spiny part refers to the spines that cover the outside of these animals. Many have a spiny skin, but some of these animals are leathery-skinned. There are approximately 6,000 species.

Body Plan

    An echinoderm's body plan is radially symmetrical. **Radial symmetry** means circular in shape. The body is a hub, like a bicycle wheel, and the outstretched arms are spokes coming out of it. Many echinoderms like the starfish, have five arms coming out from the center. In the middle, underneath its body, is a mouth. Most echinoderms have two rows of tiny feet on the bottom of each **ray** (arm). These are called **tube feet** and act like suction cups. The starfish uses its tube feet to move by filling the tube feet with water from its **water vascular system**. The water vascular system is a series of water-filled canals. As the water moves into and out of the tube feet, the echinoderm is able to move and feed. Echinoderms do not have circulatory, respiratory, or excretory systems. They have a nervous system but do not have a brain.

Classification of Echinoderms
Sea Stars

    Most starfish eat mollusks. They surround the shell and use their tube feet to pull open the two-part shell. The starfish then turns its stomach inside out by pushing its stomach through its mouth. The stomach secretes a digestive juice into the mollusk; this breaks down the soft body, and the starfish eats it like jelly. Once the starfish has digested the mollusk, it pulls its stomach back inside its body. Through regeneration, starfish can grow back arms that have been damaged or lost. **Regeneration** is a process used by some animals to replace lost or damaged body parts. Sometimes, a few severed arms can grow back into a complete starfish. However, for most starfish the arm dies.

Brittle Stars

    Brittle stars are animals that live hidden under rocks on the ocean floor. They will break off an arm as a method of defense when they feel threatened; however, they can quickly grow back the lost arm. Brittle stars move faster than the true starfish.

Sea Urchins and Sand Dollars

    Sea urchins and sand dollars are a group of echinoderms that has skeletons made of calcium carbonate plates covered with spines. The sharp spines offer protection from predators. The spines are connected to the skeleton with muscles in a manner that allows them to swivel toward a predator. Sea urchins are round and covered with long spines. Sand dollars are flat and covered with small fine spines. They have five paired rows of tube feet.

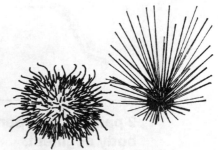

Sea Cucumbers

    A sea cucumber is a soft-bodied creature that lies on its side on the ocean floor. It has five rows of tube feet and tentacles that surround its mouth. It feeds continuously. When it feels threatened by predators, it gives up its internal organs as a method of defense. Don't worry— these expelled organs regenerate quickly.

Name: _____ Date: _____

What Is an Echinoderm? *Reinforcement Activity*

To the student observer: Circle the shape echinoderms have: **rectangular**, **circular**, **square**, or **spiral**.

Directions: Solve the puzzle below.

E _ _ _ _ _ _ _ _ _ _ _ _ _   1. _____ means "spiny-skinned."

C _ _ _   2. Tube feet act like suction _____.

H _ _ _ _ _   3. Brittle stars like to live _____ under rocks on the ocean floor.

I _ _ _ _ _ _ _ _   4. A starfish eats by turning its stomach _____ _____.

N _ _   5. Echinoderms do _____ have a brain.

O _ _ _   6. Starfish use their tube feet to _____ the shells of clams.

D _ _ _ _ _ _   7. Losing an arm is a method of _____ when threatened.

E _ _ _ _ _ _ _ _ _ _ _   8. _____ have radial symmetry.

R _ _ _ _ _ _ _ _ _ _   9. _____ means to grow back an arm.

M _ _ _ _ _ _ _   10. Many echinoderms eat _____.

S _ _ _ _ _ _ _ _ _ _ _   11. _____ _____ can expel their organs for defense.

Directions: Answer the following questions based on what you have learned about echinoderms.

12. List three characteristics of echinoderms. _____

_____

_____

13. List three examples of echinoderms.

    a. _____   b. _____

    c. _____

14. What do starfish use their tube feet for? _____

_____

15. Describe how a starfish eats. _____

_____

_____

Name: _____   Date: _____

Invertebrates Vocabulary: *Study Sheet*

To the student observer: Below is a list of important terms for the invertebrates unit. Use this list of terms and their definitions to help you complete the activities on the following pages. This study sheet will also help you prepare for the unit test.

1. **Appendages** - structures that grow from the body

2. **Closed circulatory system** - an organ system where blood moves through blood vessels

3. **Cnidocytes** - the stinging cells of cnidarians

4. **Cocoon** - a resting stage in insect development (pupa stage in metamorphosis)

5. **Endoskeleton** - a skeleton on the inside

6. **Exoskeleton** - a skeleton on the outside

7. **Invertebrate** - an animal without a backbone

8. **Larva** - the worm-like stage in insect development (caterpillar)

9. **Mantle** - a thin membrane that covers the mollusk's body

10. **Medusa** - the umbrella form of a cnidarian (tentacles hang down—jellyfish)

11. **Metamorphosis** - the changes during the life cycle (development) of an insect

12. **Molting** - the shedding of the exoskeleton

13. **Nymph** - a young insect that resembles the adult

14. **Open circulatory system** - a system where blood is not contained in vessels

15. **Polyp** - the vase-shaped form of a cnidarian (tentacles on top—sea anemones)

16. **Pupa** - a resting stage during complete metamorphosis (cocoon stage)

17. **Radula** - a rough, tongue-like organ of many mollusks

18. **Regeneration** - the ability to replace damaged or lost parts

19. **Tube feet** - the sucker-like structures on echinoderms used for movement and obtaining food

20. **Water vascular system** - a network of water-filled canals in echinoderms

Name: _____ Date: _____

Invertebrates: *Word Web*

To the student observer: Prove what you have learned about invertebrates by completing this word web. Write one of the subgroups from the word box in the correct rectangle.

Arachnids	**Arthropods**	**Cnidarians**	**Crustaceans**
Echinoderms	**Flatworms**	**Insecta**	**Mollusks**
Myriapods	**Porifera**	**Roundworms**	**Segmented Worms**

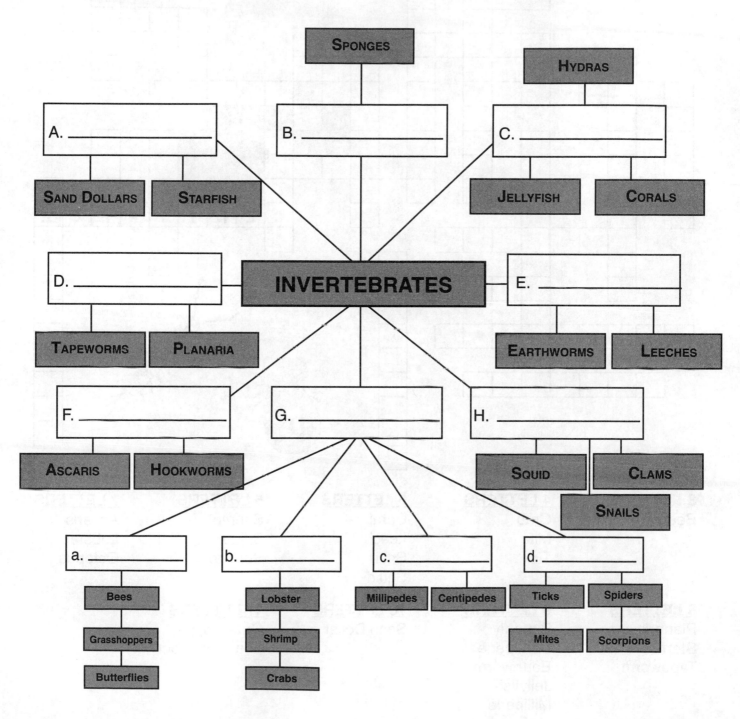

Name: _____   Date: _____

Invertebrates: *Kriss Kross*

To the student observer: An invertebrate is an animal that lacks a backbone. Most animals are invertebrates. Using a pencil, fit the words from the list below in the correct spaces. There may be two words that fit in the same boxes, but if you are unable to connect the next word, you know you have written in the wrong word. If so, then erase and continue with another word that does fit.

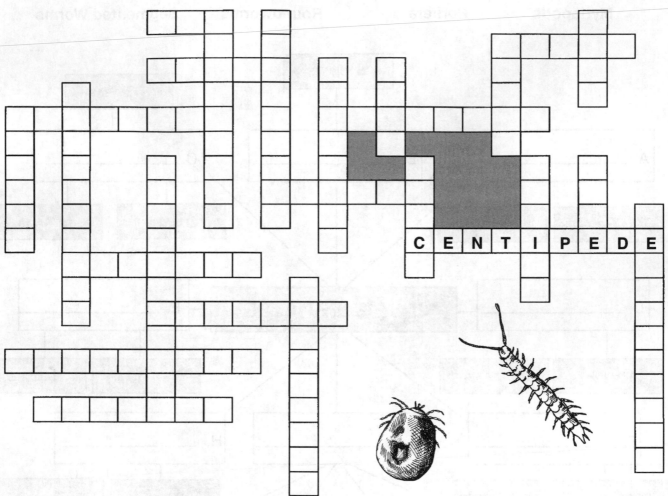

C E N T I P E D E

3 LETTERS	**4 LETTERS**	**5 LETTERS**	**6 LETTERS**	**7 LETTERS**
Bee	Crab	Coral	Shrimp	Ascaris
	Mite	Leech	Spider	Lobster
	Tick	Snail	Sponge	Octopus
		Squid		

8 LETTERS	**9 LETTERS**	**10 LETTERS**	**11 LETTERS**
Planaria	Butterfly	Sand Dollar	Grasshopper
Starfish	Centipede		Sea Cucumber
Tapeworm	Earthworm		
	Jellyfish		
	Millipede		

Name: _____ Date: _____

Invertebrates: *Crossword Puzzle*

To the student observer: An invertebrate is an animal that lacks a backbone. Most animals are invertebrates. Show what you have learned about invertebrates by completing the puzzle below.

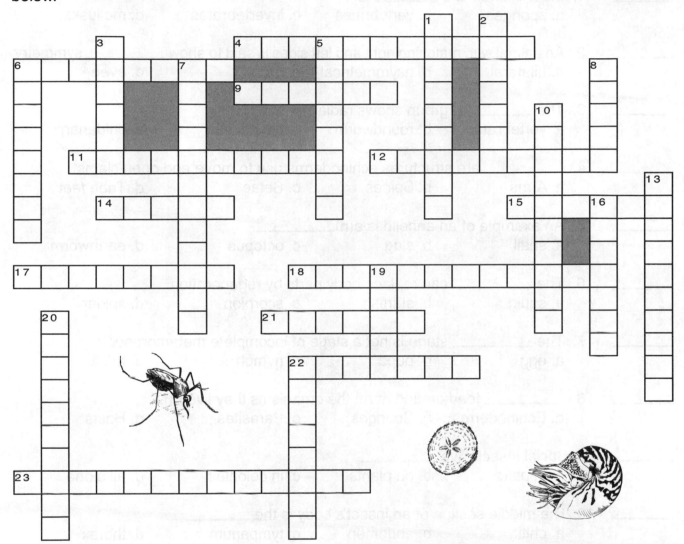

ACROSS

4. Limits the growth and size of an invertebrate
6. A long, parasitic flatworm
9. Kingdom of the invertebrates
11. A scientist who studies classification
12. A cnidarian
14. Made when sand becomes embedded in the oyster's mantle
15. Symmetry of cnidarians
17. Arthropod with eight legs
18. An animal without a backbone
21. The simplest animal
22. The shedding of the exoskeleton
23. A change in form and appearance

DOWN

1. Arm-like pieces of tissue
2. The study of animals
3. Jellyfish body form
5. An animal's arrangement of body parts
6. Roundworm associated with undercooked pork
7. A form of asexual reproduction
8. A parasitic segmented worm
10. Animals with special stinging cells
13. The only free-living flatworms
16. Largest group of arthropods
19. Number of invertebrate phyla
20. Spiny or leathery-skinned animal
22. Soft-bodied animals that usually have a shell

Name: _____ Date: _____

Invertebrates: *Unit Test*

Directions: Write the letter of the correct answer on the line at the left of the question.

_____ 1. Most animals are _____.
      a. sponges   b. vertebrates   c. invertebrates   d. mollusks

_____ 2. An animal with matching right and left sides is said to show _____ symmetry.
      a. bilateral   b. asymmetrical   c. radial   d. even

_____ 3. The _____ group shows radial symmetry.
      a. vertebrate   b. roundworm   c. crustacean   d. cnidarian

_____ 4. _____ are structures echinoderms use to move and open clams.
      a. Arms   b. Spines   c. Setae   d. Tube feet

_____ 5. An example of an annelid is a(n)_____.
      a. snail   b. slug   c. octopus   d. earthworm

_____ 6. The _____ can replace body parts by regeneration.
      a. squid   b. starfish   c. scorpion   d. spider

_____ 7. The _____ stage is not a stage of incomplete metamorphosis.
      a. egg   b. pupa   c. nymph   d. adult

_____ 8. _____ feed on and harm the organisms they live on.
      a. Echinoderms   b. Sponges   c. Parasites   d. Hosts

_____ 9. Social insects live _____.
      a. in pairs   b. on plants   c. in colonies   d. all alone

_____ 10. The middle section of an insect's body is the _____.
      a. chitin   b. abdomen   c. tympanum   d. thorax

_____ 11. The two body forms of cnidarians are Medusa and _____.
      a. polyp   b. pupa   c. nymph   d. larva

_____ 12. Oysters, squids, and octopuses are examples of _____.
      a. arthropods   b. arachnids   c. mollusks   d. echinoderms

_____ 13. Sand dollars, starfish, and sea urchins are examples of _____.
      a. arthropods   b. arachnids   c. mollusks   d. echinoderms

Name: _____ Date: _____

Invertebrates: *Unit Test (cont.)*

_____ 14. Insects, spiders, and crabs are examples of _____.
a. arthropods   b. arachnids   c. mollusks   d. echinoderms

_____ 15. _____ are simple pore-bearing animals.
a. Planarians   b. Corals   c. Sponges   d. Squid

_____ 16. _____ is a change in size and form as an animal develops into an adult.
a. Mesoderm   b. Metamorphosis   c. Regeneration   d. Osmosis

_____ 17. Arthropods have all of the following except _____.
a. jointed legs   b. segmented bodies   c. an exoskeleton   d. an endoskeleton

_____ 18. A spider can be distinguished from an insect by its _____.
a. number of legs   b. exoskeleton   c. poisonous bite   d. symmetry

_____ 19. _____ have wings, three body regions, an exoskeleton, and three pairs of jointed legs.
a. Arthropods   b. Insects   c. Spiders   d. Amphibians

_____ 20. _____ have flattened bodies with a head, tail end, three tissue layers, and most are parasites.
a. Flatworms   b. Roundworms   c. Leeches   d. Annelids

Directions: Classify these invertebrates by their phyla names. Two letters will be used twice.

_____ 21. planarians   a. porifera

_____ 22. hookworms   b. cnidarians

_____ 23. starfish   c. platyhelminthes

_____ 24. jellyfish   d. nematoda

_____ 25. leeches   e. annelida

_____ 26. sponges   f. mollusca

_____ 27. grasshoppers   g. echinodermata

_____ 28. squids   h. arthropoda

_____ 29. lobsters

_____ 30. snails

Answer Keys

A Special Group of Organisms: Reinforcement Activity (p. 5)

Observer: A vertebrate has a backbone; an invertebrate does not.

Analyze: Movement—Radial symmetry allows movement in water but would be a useless adaptation for moving on land. Matching sides work better for movement on land.

1. a. Cannot make their own food.
   b. Have many cells
   c. Have eukaryotic cells
   d. Move about
   e. Digest their food
2. An exoskeleton is on the outside of the body. An endoskeleton is on the inside of the body.
3. They molt their exoskeleton; it limits their growth.
4. Chitin is a tough, waxy, waterproof substance of which an animal's exoskeleton is composed.
5. The sponge has no symmetry.
6. a. The presence or absence of a backbone
   b. Symmetry: how their body parts are arranged

Classification: Reinforcement Activity (p. 7)

Observer: It makes identification and learning about organisms easier.

Analyze: Organisms may "appear" similar on the outside, but when the scientists look beyond appearance, they may be more similar to a different organism.

1. To put organisms into groups, based on similarities
2. Scientists classify organisms to keep track of them and to avoid errors in communication.
3. A taxonomist is a scientist who studies the science of classifying and naming living things.
4. Binomial nomenclature is a two-word naming system that gives every organism a specific scientific name.
5. A scientific name is always written in italics, with the genus name first (capitalized), and then the species name.
6. a. Physical features, external features (what the organism looks like)
   b. Cells
   c. Growth and development
   d. Blood
   e. Internal structures

What Is a Sponge?: Reinforcement Activity/Crossword Puzzle (p. 9)

Observer: The scientists observed that the sponges obtained their food by eating other organisms.

Analyze: The sponges have only two layers—no organs or systems. They are like an empty sack of cells.

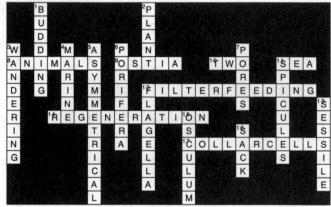

What Is a Cnidarian?: Reinforcement Activity (p. 11)

Observer: Jellyfish, hydras, corals, and sea anemones.

Analyze: The jellyfish's cells form tissue.

1. Cnidaria means "stinging cells."
2. The jellyfish shoots out poison arrows from its stinging cells, which paralyzes the prey. It then uses its tentacles to put it into its mouth.
3. A jellyfish's tentacles hang down; a sea anemone's tentacles point upward. A jellyfish's mouth is on the bottom of its body; a sea anemone's mouth is on the top of its body. A jellyfish can move over prey; an anemone is stationary, so it needs the mouth on top.

4. Digestive, muscle, nerve, and sensory
5. tentacles
6. Medusa
7. polyp
8. cnidocytes
9. food or prey
10. radial

What Is a Flatworm?: Reinforcement Activity (p. 14)

Observer: A simple worm with a flattened body that is either free-living or parasitic.

Analyze: Flatworms have bilateral symmetry, specialized organs, such as eyespots, etc., and simple systems.

1. Flatworms
2. Platyhelminthes
3. tapeworm
4. host
5. free-living
6. planarians, tapeworms, flukes
7. regenerate
8. a. endoderm
   b. mesoderm
   c. ectoderm

What Is a Roundworm?: Reinforcement Activity (p. 16)

Observer: Wear shoes when outside.

Analyze: They have a complete or continuous digestive system. (Two body openings: anus and mouth)

1. nematoda
2. free-living, parasites
3. muscle, nerve, excretory, reproductive
4. cuticle
5. continuous

Hookworm: feet, soil, intestines
Heartworm: dog, mosquito, monthly
Trichina worm: pork, rare, cysts

What Is a Segmented Worm?: Reinforcement Activity (p. 18)

Observer: Teacher: Accept any logical answer.

Analyze: They loosen the soil like a plow when they burrow.

1. advanced
2. annelida
3. coelom
4. leeches
5. setae
6. parasitic
7. rings
8. skin
9. closed
10. bristle worms

Skill Challenge:

A. hearts   B. setae   C. crop
D. gizzard   E. intestines   F. segments

What Is a Mollusk?: Reinforcement Activity (p. 22)

A. gastropod
B. cephalopod
C. bivalve

1. soft-bodied
2. shell
3. open
4. water vascular
5. radula
6. pearl
7. mantle
8. cephalopod

Skill Challenge:

Characteristics	Gastropod	Bivalve	Cephalopod
a. one shell	X		
b. two-part shell		X	
c. arms with suckers			X
d. soft, fleshy body	X	X	X
e. three body parts	X	X	X
f. well-developed head			X
g. open circulatory system	X	X	X
h. moves by jet-action			X
i. no shell			X
j. "housekeeper" for fish	X		

What Is an Arthropod?: Reinforcement Activity (p. 26)

Observer: They have adapted to life in every environment. They contain the class insecta.

Analyze: The arthropod class is too varied, and there are too many to study at the phylum level. To understand their unique traits, it is easier to study them within their classes.

1. Structures that grow from the body (i.e., arms, legs, pincers, and antennae)
2. a. jointed legs
   b. exoskeleton
   c. segmented body
3. a. head
   b. thorax
   c. abdomen
4. An exoskeleton is a skeleton on the outside. It is made of a tough, waxy substance called chitin.
5. Molting means shedding the old exoskeleton as the body grows a new one.
6. Arthropods molt in order to grow; the exoskeleton doesn't grow with the animal, it limits growth.
7. The class insecta is the largest class.
8. a. arachnids
   b. crustaceans
   c. myriapods

What Is an Insect?: Reinforcement Activity (p. 28)

Observer: Butterflies belong to class insecta.

Analyze: Yes, it aids in their survival because they work together to help the colony.

1. spiracles
2. tympanum
3. compound
4. social insects
5. a. The queen lays the eggs.
   b. The drones fertilize the eggs.
   c. The worker bees gather honey and protect the hive.

6.
Arthropods	Insects
a. jointed legs	a. 6 jointed legs
b. segmented bodies	b. 3 body regions
c. exoskeleton	c. wings, antennae

Skill Challenge: Parts of a grasshopper:
- A. abdomen
- B. thorax
- C. head
- D. antennae
- E. spiracles
- F. tympanum
- G. compound eye

How Do Insects Develop?: Reinforcement Activity (p. 30)

Observer: Teacher: Accept all logical answers.

Analyze: In complete metamorphosis, the larva stage does not resemble the adult.

1. The changes insects go through in becoming an adult; a change in body form and appearance.
2. a. complete
   b. incomplete
3. egg, larva, pupa, adult
This is called complete metamorphosis.
4. The larva stage
5. The insect spins a protective covering called a cocoon around itself, and then the insect's body is reorganized into a winged adult.
6. egg, nymph, adult
This is called incomplete metamorphosis.
7. The nymph stage
8. A. 3   B. 1   C. 4   D. 2

Other Classes of Arthropods: Reinforcement Activity (p. 32)

Observer: A spider uses its fangs to inject a poison that paralyzes its prey. It then releases an enzyme that turns the prey into liquid. The spider then sucks the liquid up.

Analyze: A centipede has only one pair of legs per segment, a poison claw, and a flattened body. A millipede has two pairs of legs per segment, is much slower than a centipede, and has a rounded body. They both have long bodies divided into many sections, jointed legs, and antennae.

1. largest
2. book
3. arachnids
4. eight
5. spiders, scorpions, mites, ticks
6. Crustaceans
7. crabs, shrimp, lobsters
8. molt
9. regenerate
10. chilopods, diplopods

Name That Arhropod: Reinforcement Activity (p. 33)

A. Arachnid
B. Arachnid
C. Insect
D. Insect
E. Arachnid
F. Crustacean
G. Diplopod
H. Crustacean
I. Chilopod

What Is an Echinoderm?: Reinforcement Activity (p. 35)

Observer: circular

1. Echinodermata
2. cups
3. hidden
4. inside out
5. not
6. open
7. defense
8. echinoderms
9. regenerate
10. mollusks
11. sea cucumbers
12. Any three: tube feet, spiny-skinned, radial symmetry (circular shape), water vascular system
13. Any three: starfish, sea cucumber, sea urchin, and sand dollar
14. For movement and for opening shells for food

15. A starfish uses its tube feet to pry open an oyster and turns its stomach inside out through its mouth. It then secretes a digestive juice that breaks down the mollusk. When finished, it lets go.

Invertebrates: Word Web (p. 37)

A. Echinoderms
B. Porifera
C. Cnidarians
D. Flatworms
E. Segmented worms
F. Roundworms
G. Arthropods
H. Mollusks
a. Insecta
b. Crustaceans
c. Myriapods
d. Arachnids

Invertebrates: Kriss Kross (p. 38)

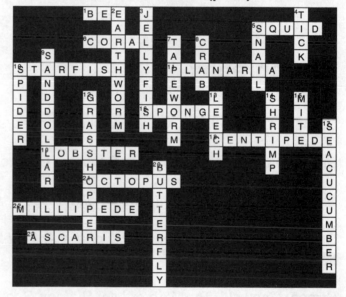

Answer Keys (cont.)

Invertebrates: Crossword Puzzle (p. 39)

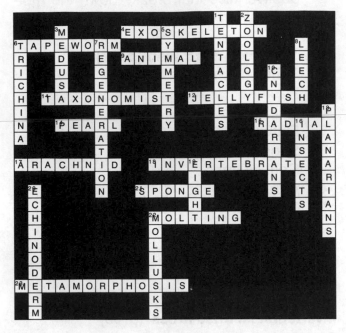

Invertebrates: Unit Test (p. 40)

1. c	2. a	3. d	4. d
5. d	6. b	7. b	8. c
9. c	10. d	11. a	12. c
13. d	14. a	15. c	16. b
17. d	18. a	19. b	20. a
21. c	22. d	23. g	24. b
25. e	26. a	27. h	28. f
29. h	30. f		

Bibliography

Bernstein, Schachter, Winkler, Wolfe. *Concepts and Challenges in Life Science*. Globe 1991.

Biggs, Daniel, and Ortleb. *Life Science*. Glencoe/McGraw-Hill, 1997.

Mound, Laurence. *Eyewitness Books: Insects*. Alfred A. Knopf, 1990.

Stidworthy, John. *Encyclopedia of the Animal World: Simple Animals.* Facts on File Publications, 1990.

Strass, Lisowski. *The Web of Life: Biology.* Scott Foresman-Addison Wesley, 2000.

World Book's Young Scientists: Animals. World Book Inc., 1995.

SCHOOL & CARNIVAL
SUPPLIES